Life Means What?

Life Means What?

J. John

Marshalls

Marshalls Paperbacks
Marshall Morgan & Scott
3 Beggarwood Lane, Basingstoke,
Hants, RG23 7LP, UK

First published by Marshall Pickering Ltd.

Reprinted : Impression number
87 88 89 90 : 10 9 8 7 6 5 4 3 2

British Library CIP Data

John, J.
  Life means what?
  1. Theology, Doctrinal
  I. Title
  230   BT77.3

  ISBN 0-511-01181-5

Typeset by Alan Sutton Publishing Ltd., Gloucester
Printed in Great Britain by
Hazell Watson & Viney Limited,
Member of the BPCC Group, Aylesbury, Bucks

To Andy Economides for introducing me
to The Way, The Truth and The Life.

Contents

Preface

I have tried to make this book as readable as possible . . . but you will never know unless you read it yourself! If you have read this far . . . then *do* read the rest.

Many ideas expressed in this book are not original – they have been picked up here and there across the years. Thank you to all those I have had conversations with and thank you to all the writers and publishers for the books I have read and been influenced by.

Special thanks to the following individuals:

To Debbie Thorpe who asked me to write the book. To Estelle Keogh, Father Thomas and Lois Thompson for their friendship, support and wisdom. To Justin Fashanu for the exceedingly lively discussions, advice and guidance. Many special thanks to Alex Lundie for the hours spent in going through the first draft, editing and suggesting. To my secretary Lin Templeman who typed and retyped the manuscript as repeated revisions were made. And my most particular thanks go to my wife, Killy, who sacrificed hours of companionship so I could write this book during my short times at home. She has been a co-operative assistant during the entire time of writing.

J. John, St. Nicholas Church, Nottingham
September 1984

1: Life Means What?

Some of the most surprising and unlikely people are sad, fearful and lonely. Some people show it, others cover it up. Other people seem happy but are not really content with life. . . . Is there something more? they ask. Is there?? Are we obsessed with acquiring things, filling our lives with things to compensate for the way we feel? Do we have goals? What are they? A good career, a big salary, ambitions to reach the top? What if you do get there? What if you don't? What does it cost?

Many people think that money is the answer to everything. Aristotle Onassis in an interview shortly before his death said 'Money does not make you happy'. The film *Citizen Kane* gives a vivid image of what happens when a person has based his life on the possession of things. The multi-millionaire Charlie Kane (played by Orson Welles) spends his life collecting things, trying to fill an empty life. At the end of the film, after he has died, the camera pans to view all the expensive objects he has bought during his life. Through the eye of the camera we see the extreme loneliness of a life centred on possessions, material gain. Is there anything more than this?

Many people feel lonely and our society contributes strongly to such feelings. The consumer age we live in puts an emphasis on the importance of things, and rapidly changing fashions and technology create a constant pressure to acquire the latest, the newest and the best. People are encouraged to judge themselves by the things they possess. We are so inundated by advertising that we often fail to understand what it is saying. It may be telling me I am what I possess, and giving me a dangerously false self-image. A steady diet of advertising can strongly influence both our consciousness and our conscience. We can start judging people by their possessions . . . their financial success, their home, their wardrobe or the size and price of their car. Why does advertising have such an effect on us? It has an impact on us because advertising plays on the one need each of us has, which is to be loved. Use this mouthwash, wear this bra, buy this perfume and you *will be* lovable, accepted, wanted.

So what *is* life all about? Just a dream as some have said? We all have aspiring dreams especially when we are younger, directing a film in our minds of what we will be like in the future and all the things we will see, do and own. I remember dreaming at school (probably during a Maths class!) about being successful, achieving everything and therefore being happy and satisfied. But if the link between success and happiness is true, then why are there so many successful people in the world who are unhappy? Raquel Welch in an interview said:

'I had acquired everything I wanted, yet I was totally miserable. . . . I thought it was very peculiar that I had acquired everything I had wanted as a child, wealth, fame and accomplishment in my career. I had beautiful children, and a lifestyle that seemed terrific, yet I was totally and miserably unhappy. I found it very frightening that one could acquire all these things and still be so miserable.'

So many other people like Raquel Welch seem to have acquired everything that they ever wanted and in the process lost what they ultimately wanted to achieve . . . could we call it fulfilment and peace? It seems so strange that other people like Mother Teresa who own nothing except one change of clothing portray such serenity and joy. Despite working with the destitute and dying, the mentally handicapped, alcoholics, drug addicts, aborted and abandoned babies, Mother Teresa says, 'I have found the paradox that if I love until it hurts, then there is no hurt, but only more love. As I held and fed the morsel of life that was an aborted baby, as I held the hand of a man dying from cancer and felt his trust and gratitude, I could see, feel and touch God's love which has existed from the beginning.'

But as some would say, 'Surely God doesn't come into it?' It's interesting that atheists like Bertrand Russell, with brilliant minds plus wealth, were dissatisfied with life and wrote often about anguish, loneliness, emptiness and lack of peace. Could it be therefore that God or God's love as Mother Teresa put it really does come into it? Katharine Tait, Bertrand Russell's daughter, wrote a book entitled *My Father Bertrand Russell* and in it she wrote:

'Somewhere at the back of my father's mind and at the bottom of his heart, in the depths of his soul, there was an empty space that had once been filled by God and he never found anything else to put in it.'

Quite an admission to make about one's famous atheist father!

So what are *your* dreams? Have they been reached? In Arthur Miller's play *Death of a Salesman*, the central character Willy Loman spends most of his life waiting to become a success and sees his road to success through the superficial relationships he develops in his work as a salesman. Whether he is urging his son to be a popular football star in school or asking his next door neighbour what the secret of success is, Willy reveals his false set of values. When he is on a sales trip Willy commits adultery, and is caught by his son, and receives no sympathy from the boy when he confesses, 'She's nothing to me, Biff – I was lonely, I was terribly lonely.' At the end of the play, at Willy's graveside, Biff sums up Willy's problem:

'He had the wrong dreams. All, all wrong.'

Willy like the rest of us, wanted and needed to be accepted, to belong, but didn't really know how to achieve it. One of the deepest needs of the human heart is the need to be appreciated. We all want to be valued. This is not to say that everybody wants to hear how wonderful they are, though no doubt some do! But every human being wants to be loved.

What a complex word love is! For some people, love is something passionate, for others it is romance, for others it is something sexual. However, there is a deeper love, the kind which accepts us as we are, which Willy in Arthur Miller's play seemed to be looking for, and which we all need too. The Bible says that's what God's love is like. I am accepted by God as I am and not as I should be. I never am as I should be. I know in reality I do not walk a straight path. There are many deceptive bends, many wrong decisions in the course of life which have brought me to where I am now. St. Augustine said, 'A friend is someone who knows everything about you and still accepts you.' That is a dream we all share: that one day I may meet the person to whom I can really talk, who understands me, who can listen and even hear what I leave unsaid, and then really *accepts* me. The God of the Bible is the fulfilment of this dream for many people all over the world.

The French philosopher Sartre wrote in his autobiography, *Les Mots*, of a boyhood experience which later had incalculable consequences. In the middle of an innocent prank he suddenly realized 'God sees me'. This so frightened him that at the very same moment he made a deliberate choice to curse God. In later years he admitted that without this misunderstanding he and God could have got along all right.

But if there is a God, why be afraid that he sees us? The idea of God or anyone else for that matter, knowing all the things we hate to admit to ourselves, terrifies us, because it is so hard to believe that anyone could accept us exactly as we are. The Bible says God loves me with my ideals and disappointments, my sacrifices and my pleasures, my successes and my failures.

This chapter seems to be filled with lots of questions. But the questions 'Who are we?', 'What are we doing here?' and, 'How much are we worth?' are important and need to be aired to fully understand and appreciate the consequences of what we do or don't do, of what we feel and think. To some, the question may not be so much 'Why am I here?' as, 'How do I get out of this mess?!'

Some would say it doesn't matter. Pyschologists like Freud tell us that our actions are the result of various repressed sexual tendencies. Sociologists like B.F. Skinner argue that all our choices are determined by social conditioning and that our freedom is an illusion, and biologists like Francis Crick regard man as just an electro-chemical machine. If these answers are right we are nothing but a miscarriage of nature, thrust into a purposeless universe to live a purposeless life. Are we to live empty lives and then die? Merely being alive does not make existence meaningful.

One of the most widely honoured and often quoted men at the turn of the century was Samuel Langhorne Clemens, better known by his pen name, Mark Twain. A man with exceptional wit and skill with words, his life was characterized by misery, cheerlessness and a tendency to expect the worst and see gloom in all things. Although most of his writings were humorous, his biographers all agree he was not a happy man, despite being loaded with so much talent. In his autobiography he wrote:

'A myriad of men are born, they labour and struggle and sweat for bread, they squabble and scold and fight, they scramble for little mean advantages over each other. Age creeps upon them and infirmities follow, shame and humiliation bring down their pride and vanities.

Those they love are taken from them, and the joy of life is turned to aching grief. The burden of pain, care, misery grows heavier year by year. At length ambition is dead, longing for relief is in its place. It comes at last – the only unpoisoned gift earth has for them – and they vanish from a world where they achieved nothing, where they were a mistake and a failure and a foolishness, where they left no sign that they had ever existed – a world that will lament them a day and forget them forever.'

Mark Twain summed it up in a simpler way in his book *The Mysterious Stranger* published in 1916, six years after his death. It has the line, 'Life is all a dream – a grotesque and foolish dream'.

Adding up what all these people are saying, mankind is no more significant than a swarm of mosquitoes or a barnyard of pigs, if their end is the same. The same blind cosmic process that coughed them up in the first place will eventually swallow them again. Unless of course there is an answer, and life *is* more than sexual tendencies, conditioning influences and electro-chemicals. Let's say that the God of the Bible does exist, and he's actually got something to say about life. . . . Just for a moment consider the consequences if he has the answers to life and we don't know anything about him!

We would have to say that Mark Twain, Bertrand Russell, men with great minds, quick wits, real literary gifts, were men without God. Talented men, now dead, who missed life's best! Thinking of death . . .

2: Only Death?

There is no human experience that frightens us so much as death. The prospect of death raises all the important questions. What, if anything, does my life mean? Is there any goal or purpose to my life? Was Shakespeare's Macbeth right in summing up all human existence as 'a tale told by an idiot full of sound and fury signifying nothing'? Is there anything more, or is death the end?

Despite the modern advancements in science and medicine, we are helpless before it. In the crypt of St. Leonard's Church, Hythe, Kent, hundreds of visitors come each summer to stare at 500 neatly shelved skulls and 8,000 femur bones stacked carefully beside them. These human remains challenge healthy young tourists with the unspoken certainty: 'As we are, so you will soon be.' Looking at a display of bones, it is hard to picture the exhibits as people who once lived, loved, laughed and cried like us. Is that it? Is death the only certainty in life? St. Augustine said long ago: 'Everything in our life, good or bad, is uncertain, except death, only death is certain.' Of course this is a simple truth known to man from the beginning of time, but the truth of it doesn't always hit us.

In the past few years there have been more books written about this subject than for a full century before.

Magazines report the long discussions of learned people on death, as well as the drawn-out courtroom debates on a suffering person's right to die. The subject of death has suddenly become a 'hot item'. Of course anyone who chooses to write about death is at an obvious disadvantage because he has never gone through the experience about which he is writing. As I have said we all know that we must die, but the delusion of many is that they imagine death as far-off, as if it will never come. There are people who at least for some period of time in their lives do not seem to take death seriously. During the 1960's life seemed so full of fun and hope for many young people that they were uninterested in the subject, not just lacking belief in life after death, but not caring whether death really was the end of human existence. Though some people laugh and shrug their shoulders, eventually the loss of a friend or someone in the family forces them into some straight thinking about death, and the conclusions they reach can entirely change their lives.

One thing is sure, which Job in the Old Testament knew, 'Man born of woman is short-lived and full of trouble. Like a flower that springs up and fades . . .' When Philip II, King of Spain, was dying, he called for his son and pulling aside his royal robes, showed the young prince the horrible sores covering his body 'See', he said, 'how even Kings die and how the grandeurs of this world end.' Death runs to meet us, and we at every moment are moving towards death. Every step, every breath, brings us nearer to the end of life. I have often wondered how those who do not think about the shortness of life and are consequently unprepared for death act in the face of it. Life *is* short and death makes what we think are the 'good things' of life appear as they really are. Of what use are any of them when all that remains for a person is the darkness of the grave? Many of us, because it terrifies us, try to avoid the questions posed by death. But surely death is the most illuminating experience we can consider in our efforts at finding meaning to life. We cannot either discover or give a meaning to life unless we first find a meaning to death. Death provides a hinge for the meaning of life. True values become clear in the light of death. Our standpoint on death is central to our standpoint on life, and both involve belief, or call for acts of faith.

We say people *die*. The key question is what is the meaning of death? What has become of the *dead* person? Most cultures say that death means the end of the person. The only survival that society seems to allow a dead individual is in the evidence of the deeds he accomplished before death or in the memory of those who knew him. See what death does to a person; before death he might have been loved, admired, even sought after; at death he is a body that must be got rid of and quickly buried in the earth.

It may be comforting to hope with Tennessee Williams that 'Death is one moment and life is so many of them', but such a conception is false, even in its physical sense. To many, death comes only at the end of an agonizingly protracted illness, the outcome of which has been written clearly on the wall for years. The slow erosion of the body resulting from dread diseases of the nervous system like multiple sclerosis or Parkinson's disease is no 'short-time' passing, either for the victims or for those who have the responsibility for caring for them.

What is the *fact* of death? The Oxford English Dictionary defines it as 'the final cessation of the vital functions'. Put simply, the fact of death is that an individual's heart stops beating and his brain stops functioning. A doctor after examination concludes, 'he is dead'. All that the doctor means is that the physical signs that we associate with human life are no longer present. But does that person cease to exist because his heart stops beating and his brain waves cease?

Why does death rock the mourners? Why do we long that there should be something more? Whether the deceased is a six year old or a sixty year old, death devastates the mourners. The question 'Why'? naturally arises. Death seems to be a mistake, an error. It's not fair. It's as though something has become fouled up in the evolutionary process. Plants and animals die and that seems natural, but not people – people *shouldn't* die. Shakespeare's King Lear articulated a universal human reaction to death when, with his dead daughter in his arms, he cried,

> 'No, no, no life!
> Why should a dog, a horse have life,
> And thou no breath at all?'
>
> (Act 5, Scene 3)

If there is something after death and life does not cease just because the heart has stopped beating, then the point of death is not a good time to deal with the issue. Businessmen will always take prudent measures in ample time to acquire financial gains in the event of loss later on. Sick people do not put off taking the medicines needed to preserve or to restore their health. A person on trial for his life will not delay preparation for his trial until the day of the trial itself. The issue of life and death are important and need looking at *now*. 'The time is short . . . the world as we know it is passing away' (1 Corinthians 7.29–31).

3: Is there a God?

– God Who?!

Is there an answer to this final problem? Yes there is. God has something to say. Before you switch off, be careful you don't reject something you don't really know much about. So many people have false, preconceived ideas about God and Jesus Christ and refuse to consider whether there is any truth in Christianity at all.

According to the Bible, and to millions of people throughout the world, God is alive and well. The Bible tells us a lot about him and about us, particularly in our relationship with him. But 'Men have forgotten God' as Solzhenitsyn put it recently. The good news is God has not forgotten us. This is the nutshell of the book of Genesis. It is easy to skip Genesis, to call it naive and unsophisticated, perhaps a little childish and certainly not scientific. But can you imagine any better way of teaching the world – educated and uneducated, the fundamental facts of its relation to the Creator? And remember that the book of Genesis doesn't really deal so much with *how* the world came into being but rather *why* it came into being. To the author of Genesis it doesn't matter whether it took a zillion years or whether it was zapped! This God seen in Genesis and the rest of the Bible is *personal*. That means he doesn't just treat me like one amongst millions, but because *he* is personal, he relates to *me* personally (that's of course if I want him to). But as well as being personal he is also very powerful, much more powerful than most of us think. So often people attempt to limit God. You can't do that, because you cannot lessen his power by what you think or feel. As well as that he is a perfect God. Perfect . . . complete, faultless, immaculate, flawless, supreme, beyond all comparison. And still these words are inadequate to explain his perfection.

However the Bible makes it clear that mere knowledge *about* God is not the same as knowledge *of* God. Knowing things about a famous person is not the same as knowing that person. The New Testament declares,

'Even the demons believe there is one God – and tremble with fear, because they do not experience God's salvation.' (James 2.19)

It is possible to acknowledge that God exists without having a relationship with God, to know *about* God and yet not *know* him. However, the Bible does reveal we can know God personally and how to go about getting to know him!

Many people all over the world do of course believe and know this personal, perfect and powerful God, yet many do not. For many there are problems with believing in God. Something that confuses and bewilders people often is the question 'If God is all-knowing, all-loving and all-powerful, then why is there so much suffering in the world all the time?' 'Why the pain? Why are ordinary people in the world at this moment facing starvation? Something like 25 million will die this year because they do not have enough to eat. Why are innocent people blown up by bombs or run over by cars or struck by some illness or crippled by some accident?' 'Why doesn't God seem to care? Why doesn't God do something?'

'Why didn't he do something when 6 million Jews were driven into the gas chambers by Hitler?'

'Is there a God?' If there is, is he in control of this world? and if he is, how can he be God?

In 1964 an avalanche of coal-slag engulfed a school and part of a small mining town in Wales – killing 144 people: 116 of them children.

Aberfan.

Shortly after the Aberfan disaster, the magazine *Punch* published an editorial headed, 'Should God Resign?'

The Chairman of the Coal Board offered to resign. *Punch* responded, 'God's at the top, he's responsible, he should resign.'

Of course if God were not a good and loving God there would not be any problem at all about suffering. Most other religions in the world accept the fact of suffering with resignation because they see their deities as infinitely remote from the problems and sufferings of this world, and consider suffering as a direct response for their sin or failure. They see their gods as impersonal, detached and totally unfeeling. But the God of the Bible, the Father of Jesus Christ is revealed as a good, loving, personal God. If he is good and loving, then where is he and what's he doing?

Well, first let's look at some of our ideas about him. Our ideas of God are often defined and determined by what we want or what suits us. Maybe, a 'Grand Old

Man' – old, senile, easily fooled, demanding little, benevolent, to be patronized and played with. Maybe a lucky charm who protects us or should protect us from problems, pains and the harsher realities of life. Some see him as a cruel and punishing judge, playing with our lives and emotions like a heavenly puppeteer. Others only accept God on their own terms or demand drama and sensation. Usually people form ideas and pictures of God that keep him at a distance, with no bearing on or relevance to daily life or find for themselves excuses to ignore him. One image of God that many people have is like the portrait conveyed in a Beatles song, 'He's a real nowhere man, sitting in his nowhere land, making all his nowhere plans for nobody.'

You don't have to rack your brain to grind up some great original idea about God. All you have to do is to start looking for him quietly through the pages of the Bible where he is shown as a living God, reaching out to people in history and today. God is not just a mechanical life-force. He is the one who loves us and wants us to enjoy a special kind of relationship with him.

The Christian writer Tolstoy in his book *War and Peace* wrote, 'All, everything that I understand, I understand only because I love.' We understand and believe in others because we love them and God understands and believes in us because he loves us.

However God is not only a personal God but also infinite in all dimensions and aspects; therefore his wisdom and ways of working are infinitely greater than our own.

Isaiah 55. 8, 9 says,

'"My thoughts" says the Lord, "are not like yours, and my ways are different from yours. As high as the heavens are above the earth, so high are my ways and thoughts above yours".'

Yet so many people try exactly to limit God to their own comprehension and are left with a comfortable yet ineffective, irrelevant and powerless image of God.

A lesson that Job in the Old Testament had to learn was that it's no good shaking your fist at God and saying to God 'You first satisfy my questions, before I will believe in you' – because that is proud and arrogant. God does not have to justify himself to us. As the Living Bible puts it in Psalm 111.10,

'How can men be wise? The only way to begin is by reverence for God.'

Man is not at the centre of the universe with *God* on trial. God is at the centre of the universe with *man* on trial. And man, frankly speaking has made a real mess of things.

Which is the true-to-life picture: the man of distinction and the God who is dead? Or the man who is alienated and the God who is really there?

Although the Old Testament shows God to be beyond definition and total understanding it does show him as a living God acting and revealing himself in creation and in history. He is a moving Spirit but cannot be seen, eternal yet personal. The compassionate God, he it is who has chosen to be God-with-us, and has revealed himself in Jesus. The evangelist Matthew, after describing the birth of Jesus, writes:

'Now all this took place to fulfil the words spoken by the Lord though the prophet: "The virgin shall conceive and give birth to a son and they will call him Immanuel," a name which means, God-is-with-us.'　　　　　　　　　　(Matthew 1.22–23)

4: Jesus Christ

or

Jesus The Christ?

Many writers and artists have tried to face the question, 'Who is Jesus Christ?' and communicate his significance for each generation. Despite our critical generation, which has shattered the reputations of many great personalities of the past, Jesus Christ remains a dominant figure. There is no denying the importance of Jesus of Nazareth in the history of mankind and in the lives of at least a thousand million people in the world today, who call him by such titles as Lord, Saviour, son of God.

Time magazine described him (June 21, 1971) as 'the most persistent symbol of purity, selflessness and brotherly love in the history of western man.' Even the atheist H.G. Wells, a historian, has made this admission, as if, in spite of himself, he must recognize something about Christ. 'I am an historian, I am not a believer. But this penniless preacher from Galilee is irresistibly the centre of history.' This observation is literally quite true. He has walked through the last 2000 years of history, of empires, governments, political systems and philosophies and has remained a dominant, challenging yet mysterious personality.

Yet many today do not believe in him and for many Christianity is a joke-subject. Maybe you are such a person and have never honestly and intelligently looked at the person of Jesus Christ. Well, how about taking him seriously?

Where do we start? I am aware of how much there is to say about Christ and I am reminded of the rhyme of the five wise men of Hindustan, who went to see the elephant though each of them was blind. One grabbed the tail and thought an elephant was like a rope, another took a foot and thought the animal was like a tree, another bumped into the side and thought it was like a wall and so on. The obvious conclusion about the wise men who disputed loud and long, each in his argument, exceeding stiff and strong was that each was partly in the right and each was in the wrong!

Before we look at the Jesus in the Bible, let's look at some people's ideas about him, past and present. There is a tendency to remake Jesus and concoct the kind of Jesus who is liveable with, to project somebody who satisfies the individual's own desires, ambitions and prejudices.

In Milton's *Paradise Regained* we find an intellectual Christ, who rejects the common people as a

'herd confus'd, a miscellaneous rabble who extol things vulgar.'

How can this be? We know that Jesus made an impact on the world of his time. And that the ordinary people heard him gladly. And you must remember that the ordinary people ('the people of the land') formed more than 90 per cent of the total Jewish population of Palestine.

They were the 'people of the land', peasants, craftsmen, farmers, fishermen, who formed the majority of the population outside the cities, which were mainly Greek in culture . . . 'Rejected the common people'?! Impossible!

For D.H. Lawrence, the resurrection could be connected with Jesus' awakening sexual desires. In the winter season of 1977 a small theatre in Munich put on a play with a brothel as its setting. A brothel customer dressed up as Christ walked across the stage carrying a cross. Another wearing bishop's robes sang hymns to nude prostitutes.

In Denmark the script of the pornographic Jesus film by Jens Thorsen has already appeared in print. Publication of the English version and production of the film have so far been prevented in other countries, although Thorsen has constantly been making strong attempts to complete his project for years now.

It seems so strange that Thorsen and Lawrence and others like them swayed so far from the truth about Jesus. Jesus, in Matthew 5, said, 'You have heard that it was said, Do not commit adultery. But now I tell you, anyone who looks at a woman and wants to possess her is guilty of committing adultery with her in his heart. So if your right eye causes you to sin take it out and throw it away! It is much better for you to lose a part of your body than to have your whole body thrown into hell. If your right hand causes you to sin, cut it off and throw it away! It is much better for you to lose one of your limbs than for your whole body to go to hell.' Jesus' teaching was sharp and strong, not only against carrying out a wrong sexual action, but even against the *thought* of it. How could one who taught *against* lust and adultery be considered as an ideal character for a film based on them?!

In 1980 a Dutch cast put on *Council of Love* in Hamburg. This play was a mockery of God the Father, God the Son and God the Holy Spirit. Heaven was depicted with figures staggering about on inflated fleecy clouds.

In Scotland at the Edinburgh Festival fringe a group staged *Satan's Ball*, a production portraying Christ as a pathetic insane fool sworn at by devil worshippers and finally crucified in the nude.

Walls of churches and schools in England and abroad have been smeared with slogans. The words Jesus Stinks were painted in large letters on the wall of a church in Stuttgart.

It's interesting that in Revelation 21 where a glimpse of what heaven will be like is given, it ends with verse 8 'but cowards, traitors, perverts, murderers, the immoral, those who practice magic, those who worship idols, and all liars – the place for them is the lake burning with fire and sulphur!' If there is a God and what the Bible says is true . . . then to make a mockery of God is very dangerous!

In a woman's magazine the miracle of the incarnation (God becoming man) was presented in a repulsive manner. The title of the leading article speaks for itself, *Mary, the Crafty Unmarried Mother*. The front cover shows an obviously immoral woman with a corresponding male figure in the background. By means of photomontage (the technique of producing a composite picture of combining several photographs) a representation of the child Jesus also appears on the cover, as if held in the arms of the mother.

The Bible reports that an angel visited Mary. 'The angel said to her, "Don't be afraid, Mary, God has been gracious to you. You will become pregnant and give birth to a son, and you will name him Jesus. He will be great and will be called the Son of the Most High God. The Lord God will make him a King, as his ancestor David was, and he will be the King of the descendants of Jacob for ever; his kingdom will never end!" Mary said to the angel, "I am a virgin, How then, can this be?"' Immoral?

Has what you have just read surprised you or have you ever had similar thoughts? There are indeed many false ideas and it is important to note that there are other ideas a lot more subtle than these blatantly unhistorical and untrue fantasies in the media! Jesus Christ was never like that. The Bible says that Christ was the holiest man ever born. In human form, he was the same as other men but unique in character. No man could accuse this man of sin (doing wrong).

As for other parts of the media, the films about him, (apart from the Communist Pasolini's *The Gospel According to St. Matthew*, which portrays Jesus as the defender of the oppressed proletariat) more positive spectacles began in 1927 with Cecil B. De Mille's *King of Kings*, followed by *Ben Hur*, *The Robe*, *The Greatest Story Ever Told*, and the most recent TV production by Zeffirelli, *Jesus of Nazareth*. These films (to my amazement!) are generally content to present the life of Jesus with little variation from or addition to the Biblical text.

The theatre has done otherwise, finding great success in such modern musicals as *Jesus Christ Superstar* and

Godspell. Both have in common the fact that they focus on the human Jesus – crucifying but not resurrecting their hero. How can there be any Christianity without the resurrection? The resurrection is the centre of Christianity. It's the lynchpin: if you pull it out the whole thing will collapse. No Christ, no Christianity. Perhaps this reflects the limits of belief amongst many people in our society today – Jesus, a man who died on a cross.

Superstar, which was one of the largest selling albums in musical history, concentrates on the last seven days of Christ's mortal life with its basic question 'Who are you, Jesus?' The Jesus of *Superstar* speaks to the need of many in today's world – he is the symbol of peace and brotherhood, but he is shown to be no more than a good man, who was bullied by the establishment and executed by the lovers of war. It is a human Jesus ('he is just a man' is repeated over and over), he is like a pop idol tired from the persistent demands of his fans, the superficial crowds, ('Hey, Jesus won't you smile at me') the taunting Herod ('Walk across my swimming pool').

What a contrast to what the Bible says about him! The Bible speaks of him as the mighty God, Lord, King, Life, Light, Astonishing, Amazing.

Just a man?! No way.

5: This Jesus

History is full of men who have claimed that they came from God, or that they were gods, or that they bore messages from God – Buddha, Jesus, Confucius, Mohammed and thousands of others. Each of them has a right to be heard and considered, but how do we decide whether any of them or all of them are right in their claims? It seems to me that two good tests would be reason and history. Reason because everyone has it and history because everyone lives in it and therefore should know something about it.

Reason suggests to me that if any one of these men actually did come from God, the least God could do would be to support the messenger's claim and so support him by pre-announcing his coming! Car manufacters tell the public when to expect a new model. If God sent anyone from himself, or came himself with an important message for the world, it would seem reasonable that he would first let us know when his agent was coming, where he would be born, where he would live, what he would teach, the enemies he would make, and the manner of his death. Therefore by the extent to which the agent met with these announcements, we could judge the validity of his claims. Reason further suggests that if God did not do this, then there would be nothing to prevent any impostor from appearing in history and saying, 'I come from God'. In such cases there would be no objective, historical way of testing the messenger. We would have only his word for it, and he could be wrong!

If a visitor came to England and said he was a diplomat, the government would ask him for his passport and other documents testifying that he represented a certain government. If such proofs of identity are asked from delegates of other countries, reason certainly ought to do so with messengers who claim to have come from God. To each claimant reason says, 'What record was there before you were born that you were coming?' There were no predictions about Buddha or Mohammed, but with Christ there were. In the Old Testament one finds clearly predicted the virgin birth of the Messiah, the prophecy of Isaiah 53 about the patient sufferer, the Servant of the Lord, who would lay down his life and many other prophecies. The Old Testament speaks of one to come. If one searches the Old Testament to discover the references relating to this person to come, can one doubt that the ancient predictions point to Jesus? No! Why? Because Jesus fulfilled every single prophecy.

Not only this but when Jesus appeared, he struck history with such impact that he split it in two, dividing it into two periods, one before his coming, the other after it. Even those who deny God must date their attacks upon him A.D. so and so!

Another interesting fact separating him from all other 'leaders' is that every person who ever came into this world came into it to live. Jesus came into it to die. Death was a stumbling block to Socrates – it interrupted his teaching. But to Christ, death was his goal and the new beginning. Few of his words are really understood without reference to his cross. From the moment the soldiers rolled the stone across the door of the tomb, they thought his 'movement' was doomed. But that was not the case! It continued and grew after his resurrection. The scattered and bewildered band of his disciples gathered together and through their belief in him, the message of Jesus Christ spread. The message of GOOD NEWS. Jesus came as a Saviour, not merely as teacher. It meant nothing to teach men to be good unless he also gave them the power to be good, after rescuing them from the power of death.

For two thousand years now, Jesus of Nazareth has been the cause of divergent opinions. Some of his fellow Jews looked on him as a scandal. Some Greeks wrote him off as foolish, 1 Corinthians 1.23 'but we preach Christ crucified, a stumbling block to Jews and foolishness to Gentiles'. Even some of his relatives thought he was out of his mind. Yet he was also admired, loved and adored by many. He is the reason why Christianity is alive and thriving in the world today. Although he scarcely ever went beyond the confines of his own land, his teachings have influenced the thinking and the lives of millions throughout the world. This is all the more remarkable because from a human point of view he was a public failure and died a disgraceful death. Despite this, Jesus of Nazareth is indeed fascinating and without doubt the most important person the world has ever seen. He transcends the categories into which famous people fit. Of the many famous men and women that have come and gone in the course of history, some are vaguely remembered and many entirely forgotten. By contrast Jesus Christ is very much alive. He never wrote a book yet in the last century alone over sixty thousand books have been written about him. Has his attraction anything to do with family connections? Of course not! He was born in an obscure village, the child of a peasant woman and grew up on a tiny strip of land along the eastern shore of the Mediterranean, of no particular resources or value except as a land bridge between Mesopotamia and Egypt.

Taking a closer look at this Jesus

Jesus Christ was very normal and ordinary, at times weary, but always very human. In John 4 the story describes Jesus arriving at a well in Samaria, and having to sit down because he was so tired. Sometimes we meet people who seem to be able to constantly rush about and not get tired, and still have lots more energy left, Jesus was certainly not like that. It is noteworthy that in fact the very actions that he was most frequently criticized for were the actions which actually showed him most as a man. When John the Baptist, the messenger sent to prepare the way for Jesus, came preaching, the crowds noticed that he did not drink and did not eat what they ate, so they complained that he was too severe. Yet when Jesus came eating and drinking with the people, they said, 'Look at this man! He is a glutton and a drinker, a friend of tax collectors and sinners.'

We seem so ready to accept a Christ who was never disturbed and never angry, yet this is not the picture presented in the Gospels. In the Gospels we see a man whose indignation at times blazes forth even against his own disciples. For example when Peter said to Jesus that the things he had just been talking about should not happen. Jesus did not hesitate to reprove him, 'Get

38

behind me Satan'. His indignation was spontaneous and very obvious when he reproved his disciples for holding back the people who were bringing to him their children, 'Let the little children come to me, and do not hinder them, for the Kingdom of God belongs to such as these.'

His anger was particularly strong against those who attempted to come between God and man. 'Making a whip out of some cord, he drove them all out of the temple, cattle and sheep as well, scattered the money changers, coins, knocked their tables over, and said to the pigeon sellers, "Take all this out of here and stop turning my Father's house into a market".' (John 2.15–17)

Jesus' life had been a hard life. He never knew luxury, born in a stable and at death had nothing but the clothes on his back, and he was stripped even of these. Between these two terminals he lived a life which he summed up, 'Foxes have holes and the birds of the air have nests, but the Son of Man has nowhere to lay his head.' (Luke 9.58) On the other hand, it would be wrong to see in Christ one who did not understand human joys. Nowhere in the Gospels do we see him turning in scorn from the ordinary pleasures of life. He was having a good time at the wedding in Cana – in fact, he made more wine, gallons of it, just so that the guests could continue their celebration!

He had friends among the propertied. Nicodemus, Joseph of Arimathea, Zacchaeus, Matthew, his friends of Bethany, the wealthy ladies who 'provided for them out of their own resources' (Luke 8.3) But nowhere in the Gospels is there an indication that he sought out these wealthy friends in preference to the poor. His sensitive heart responded to human need wherever he encountered it. In Bethany he stands beside the tomb of Lazarus weeping because he has lost his friend. Human misery in any form always called forth a sympathetic response in Christ. The sick and the handicapped he took to heart, and always he was there to take the part of the poor and the oppressed. One of the most characteristic qualities of Christ was this ability of his to live for others. In the words of the Apostle Paul: 'Christ did not think of himself.' He was truly a man for others.

In many ways, it is easier to say what Jesus was not, than to put into words the unique Jesus that the Gospels describe. Schweitzer, in his book, *Jesus*, gives a very interesting title to one chapter: 'Jesus: The Man who Fits no Formula'. Our vocabulary does not seem adequate in coming to grips with the tremendous mystery that is Jesus. Jesus eludes most of our categories. History is strewn with the wreckage and skeletons of books that attempted to say the last word about Jesus of Nazareth, which presented a Jesus, in Schweitzer's words, 'Who was too small because we had forced Him into conformity with our human standards and human psychology'.

On one occasion, having fed thousands of people with five bread rolls and two small fish, Jesus satisfied their physical hunger but was aware of their inner hunger which he had come to satisfy. So he told them that the bread he would give would nourish them into life everlasting. When he told them that the true bread came down from heaven, they asked, '"Give us this bread now and always". He answered "I am the bread of life".'

This was the third time that Jesus used an image from the Old Testament to symbolize himself. The first was when he likened himself to the ladder that Jacob saw, so revealing himself as a link (a mediator) between heaven and earth. In his discussion with Nicodemus, he compared himself to the brass serpent, a symbol of healing to the Jews. Now he referred to the manna which the Hebrews had eaten and claimed that he was the true bread. Once again, he makes the shadow of the cross appear. Bread must be broken, and he who had come from God must be broken like bread that people may feed on him.

'How can this man give us his flesh to eat?' they said. Jesus replied, 'I am telling you the truth, if you do not eat the flesh of the Son of Man and drink his blood, you will not have life in yourselves. Whoever eats my flesh and drinks my blood has eternal life.' (John 6.52–54).

He not only pictured himself as one who had come down from heaven but as one who had come down to give himself to die.

On another occasion Jesus said, 'I am the light of the world'. It was not his teaching that was the light of the world, but rather his person. Just as there is only one sun to light the world physically, so he was saying that he was the only light for the world spiritually. Without him, every person would be wrapped in spiritual darkness. As dust in a room cannot be seen until the light is let in, so no one can know himself until this light shows him his true condition. Some people say that Jesus was merely a good man. A 'good man' could never claim to be the light of the world, for there would cling to him some of the trappings and faults of even the best human nature. Buddha wrote a code which he said would be useful to guide men in darkness, but he never claimed to be the light of the world. The truth that all other ethical teachers proclaimed, and the light that they gave to the world, was not *in* them, but *outside* them. Jesus however, identified himself with divine wisdom.

'I am the way, the truth and the life, no one comes to the Father except by me. If you knew me you would know my Father too.' (John 14.6, 7)

This is equivalent to saying (as somebody once said) without the way there is no going, without the truth, there is no knowing, without the life, there is no living. The way becomes real when it becomes personal to each of us. There is no such thing as seeking the truth and then finding Christ. Christ is the truth. Christ puts us back in relationship with the Father. For he is the only possible way by which God can address himself to a world of sinners.

'My Father has given me all things. No one knew the Son except the Father, and no one knows the Father except the Son, and those to whom the Son chooses to reveal him.' Matthew 11.27
Jesus said again, 'I am telling you the truth: I am the gate for the sheep. All others who came before me are thieves and robbers, but the sheep did not listen to them. I am the gate. Whoever comes in by me will be saved, he will come in and go out and find pasture. The thief comes only in order to steal, kill and destroy. I have come in order that you might have life – life in all its fullness.'
(John 10.7–10)

No one else made himself the condition of securing peace and eternal life. Jesus described himself as a door. As the old city of Troy had but one gate, so Jesus

said that he was the only gate of salvation. Salvation –
salvaged from sin, the world, the devil and death to a
new life with forgiveness and a sure hope!

When one takes into account Jesus' repeated claims
about his divinity – asking us to love him above
parents, to believe in him even in the face of persecu-
tion, to be ready to sacrifice our bodies – to call him
just a good man ignores the facts. Therefore we must
either lament his madness or adore him. The choice
that lies before us is that he either lied or he spoke the
truth.

If Christ was not all that he said he was, namely the
Son of the living God, the word of God in the flesh,
then he was not 'just a good man' – indeed he must
have been a liar, the greatest deceiver who ever lived.
If he was only a man, then he was not even a 'good'
man. But he was not only a man. He would have us
either to worship him or despise him – despise him as a
mere man, or worship him as true God and true man.
That is the alternative he presents.

If he is what he claimed to be, the Saviour, then we
have a leader worth following in these terrible times.
Jesus who stepped out of death, crushing sin, gloom
and despair, a leader to whom we can make sacrifice
without loss and from whom we gain freedom!

'There is much else that Jesus did. If it were all to
be recorded in detail, I suppose the whole world
could not hold the books that would be written.'

(John 21.25)

6: The Problem

– SIN

Qualifications for being a sinner

No other book treats sin as seriously as the Bible. So how do you qualify to be considered seriously as a sinner? Jesus Christ and others in the Bible spoke about sin and the things people have done wrong, and though nineteen centuries have come and gone, there is no real difference between sin then and sin now. What is it anyway? Sin for most people is a rather intangible fluid thing until it crystallizes into some kind of crime. But then for some people crime is crime, it is not sin, is it?

It's interesting that through the years we have tried to remove the word SIN from our vocabulary and instead we use words like crime and disease, yet there is a great difference between sin and crime. In order to be convicted for a crime, you must break some law that has been made by man, be brought to court, tried and found guilty. Only then are you a criminal. It is far more comfortable to talk about criminals than sinners. Sinners could be anywhere, but criminals are only a small percentage of the population – those people who are locked up in prisons!

It's interesting to note how the word sin has been replaced by the word crime, and more recently the word crime has been replaced by the word illness. Robbers and murderers are criminals but for society to feel that it is progressing and improving itself many of these criminals have been labelled 'sick', so the father who squanders the rent money is no longer an irresponsible drunk, but is said to have a drinking problem. People who abuse their minds with pills are now said to have a drug problem. The adulterer has a marital problem, and the criminal, whether a mugger on the street or a white collar embezzler or a tax cheat, is now called a victim of circumstances. In this scheme of things the thief and the wife beater do not deserve justice or punishment, but treatment. Yes, there are diseases and there are crimes, but 'diseases' are not crimes. Not all criminals are sick. Cheating in the school classrooms, stealing from stores, factories and banks is not obviously a symptom of illness. No one would suggest that 72 per cent of store employees and 80 per cent of bank employees are 'sick' because they steal but does that mean they are not sinners?! The advantage of course in calling sin sickness is that you do not associate guilt with sickness. If no guilt then no responsibility, then no accountability and of course no punishment. It would be thoughtless and heartless to punish sick people. The disappearance of the word SIN creates the opportunity for nobody to be responsible for wrong and the evil that has been carried out. But there must be some personal responsibility in all human acts!

Because of all this there are many people who do not know their sins and have imperfect ideas of themselves.

This is sad because until they know their sins, they cannot really come to a confession of guilt and experience forgiveness and healing. We can see the faults of others plainly enough but we cannot see our own. We get angry with those who try to make us see ourselves as we really are, and we find it hard to accept that they are right. We do all we possibly can to hide what we really are from ourselves and from others. Some people claim to be decent, good-living men and women in the world. Does it matter what a man believes provided he is 'sincere' and 'decent'? Yes it does matter! But by whose standard do we mean decent?

Jesus Christ was crucified by the ordinary sins of everyday.

Sincerity and decency are not enough. God has revealed the truth to us through Jesus Christ and the final revelation of what is good and true is seen at the Cross. A good prayer to pray is one that Job in the Old Testament prayed, 'Make me to know my sins and my wrongs' (Job 13.23). Notice that he prays 'my sins'. Some people acknowledge the fact that all people are sinners. It is as if the thought of the universality of sin makes the guilt of each person in particular less. Yes, we are all sinners but each of us needs to recognize and admit his own, then the solution to all this can also become personal.

Do we really all qualify as sinners?

According to God's law, however you try to define it, if you have failed to do what God has commanded you not to . . . it is sin. Let's forget about crime, murder and stealing because they may never concern us: most of us don't do these sort of things. All the same we still qualify. Sin, Jesus said, is not just expressed in action, but also in thought. Sin is the angry intention, stopping short of murder, or the lustful thought, stopping short of adultery, or the greedy thought and jealous thought stopping short of theft.

Sin is not just concerned with our behaviour towards others, but also with our attitude towards God. When Jesus Christ was asked what the most important commandment was, he replied, 'Love the Lord your God with all your heart, with all your soul and with all your mind. This is the greatest and the most important commandment.' Therefore if we don't keep it, we sin. It's amazing how many people think that sin means wrong use of sex i.e. pre-marital sex which in the Bible is called fornication and extra-marital sex which is called adultery. But sin is not just sexual, although fornication and adultery do come under the umbrella of sin as do theft, fraud, drunkenness, murder, hate and so on. Most people agree that these things are wrong, but the heart of the problem lies further back than these actions. The originating and the motivating factor behind them is selfishness. We look at others and see only the outward appearance and call some good and others bad. But God who sees our hearts sees us all in the same condition. We are all corrupt inside and the human heart is basically the same in every individual. Jesus said that all these wrongs come from the same source, a person's heart, 'For from the inside from a person's heart, come the evil ideas which lead him to do immoral things, to rob, kill, commit adultery, be greedy and do all sorts of evil things, deceit, indecency, jealousy, slander, pride and folly – all these evil things come from inside a person and make him unclean.'

The condition of our hearts is what's wrong with us and this is the root of the problem. Jeremiah puts it like this 'Who can understand the human heart? There is nothing else so deceitful.' The Apostle Paul knew this without a shadow of doubt: 'I know that good does not live in me – that is, in my human nature.'

How did all this start? is a question often asked. The Bible is very clear on this and says that at the beginning of the world when Adam and Eve disobeyed God and turned against him, sin entered man and death was the result. As well as this, sin and death became hereditary and therefore was passed from generation to generation.

'Sin came into the world through one man, and his sin brought death with it. As a result, death has spread to the whole human race because everyone has sinned' (Romans 5.12). In other words sin is inbred, inborn in all of us. The Bible puts it even more bluntly when in Romans 3.23, it makes it clear that no one is an exception: '. . . for all have sinned and fall short of the glory of God.' We may feel that we have to justify ourselves, because although we may acknowledge that we have sinned, we are not as bad as some people: 'I'm pretty good compared to . . .', we say. That's not the point. There may be a big difference between us and others in the *amount* of our wrongdoing, but there is no difference in the fact of their sins and ours as far as God is concerned. Because God is holy and perfect, he requires us to be that way too. He laid down a standard for us in the Ten Commandments. How many people do you know who have kept all the Ten Commandments? You may know people who have kept eight or nine of them. That is still not good enough. Jesus said that even if you only broke one in thought, in your mind, in essence, you might as well have broken them all. The amount by which we have missed the mark is quite irrelevant. We must not compare ourselves with other people, but we must compare ourselves with the perfect standards God demands. How do we match up with his laws and his standards?

This situation of sin is serious and not one to joke about because we are condemned by God and come under his judgement. The effect of sin is death both spiritual and physical. It is a separation from God. It's like a cancer, unless you do something about it, the end is certain. So do you and I qualify for sin? YES. So what we should be asking is what can be done about it, this cancerous sin?

7: The Solution – Part 1

'The last meal and then . . .'

The main dish of the last supper which Jesus ate with his disciples was the one year old lamb which Peter and John had gone on ahead to prepare. For the Jewish disciples this lamb was a reminder of the past. The passover lamb (as it was known) was in memory of the exodus from Egypt and all the powerful miracles that went with it as signs of God's faithfulness to his chosen people. For Jesus, however, this lamb was a sign which pointed into the very near future. Soon Jesus would be the lamb led to the slaughter house. The book of Leviticus in the Old Testament narrates the story of the scapegoat which was metaphorically loaded with the sins of Israel and sent into the wilderness to die. Soon Jesus would be the lamb of God, the scapegoat taking the sins of the world. Every year the high priest would go into the sanctuary of the Temple to sprinkle the ark of the covenant with sacrificial blood to obtain God's forgiveness for the sins of the people. Soon Christ would obtain forgiveness once and for all offering to God his own blood shed on the Cross. He knew full well that when he broke the bread, his own body would be broken. Did he die or was he killed? Jesus said, 'No one takes my life from me; I lay it down of my own free will'. This is what he told his disciples and after singing songs of praise after their supper they left for the Mount of Olives. Jesus led the disciples to the place where he often spent his nights: 'In the daytime he would be in the Temple teaching, but would spend the night on the hill called the Mount of Olives.'

Now imagine the scene, Jesus leaves eight of the disciples at the entrance to the garden. They have to think things out for themselves. So much has happened in so short a time! He takes with him Peter, James and John. Now for the first time Jesus is filled with fear and anguish. There is a difference between knowing something remotely and knowing the same thing close at hand. We know for instance that one day we shall die. But when a doctor says, 'You have one month to live,' our perspective of death changes. Jesus knew that the next day he would be crucified.

Several times Jesus goes to the disciples, his friends, during this night of torment. He has only asked that they sit through the long dark hours with him, but they let him down. They do love Christ but don't manage to do even the simple things he asks. They sleep and Jesus remains awake, suffering without comfort in utter distress. The disciples do not even realize that Jesus is suffering.

The guards arrive and arrest him, led to him by one of his closest friends. In the barrack yard at the back of Pilate's house Jesus' hands are tied together with a piece of rope which runs through an iron ring at the top of the pillar. The pillar is of course a high one, at least a couple of feet taller than Jesus himself. So they raise his arms above his head and therefore regulate the length of the rope in such a way that only the tips of his toes touch the ground. Jesus doesn't say anything! They beat him mercilessly, on whatever part of his body the lash chances to fall. Still he remains silent. They cut the ropes at last and Jesus collapses at the foot of the pillar – lying in his own blood. The number of strokes were deliberately limited so that death would not occur – death would come another way. This scourging was cruel and unjust. Twice over the governor publicly states that the prisoner is an innocent man! 'I find no reason to condemn this man . . . therefore I will have him whipped and set him free.' Was there ever a more illogical 'therefore' uttered? Let's imagine a scene in a modern court of law today. The person in question is in the dock, all the evidence is given. The jury retires and considers the evidence and returns with a 'not guilty' verdict. The prisoner smiles and sighs with relief (a weight off his mind), waves to his family and friends in the Court; in return they wave congratulations. The Judge stands and tells the Court, 'This man has been tried and the jury declares him innocent; I have therefore decided to sentence him to five years imprisonment.'

Unbelievable! But it happened to Jesus. Why?

Still in the barrack yard of Pilate's palace, the soldiers drag Jesus from the place he has been lying since the scourging ended. At this stage he is already dying but this is only the beginning of the suffering to come. He can scarcely stand. They take hold of his arms, one on the right and one on the left, and between them they push him along to a throne prepared for him, for he has said he is a King, hasn't he? He stumbles over it, a low stool, because the blood and tears have blinded his eyes. Laughing and mocking they robe him in scarlet. He still doesn't say a thing!

But of course how could we forget a king's crown! Oh, but we only have thorn branches to make this crown. They do not merely lay it on his head, to make certain it will stay in position they force it into place and the thorns pierce his face and head. They stand before him and bow with derisive laughter, heaping on him every insult they can devise. They come close to him and look leeringly into his face. He can feel their foul breath upon him. They strike his face and spit and blindfold him. There is no other gesture so expressive of contempt as to spit deliberately into a person's face, but why did they blindfold him? Did they feel threatened by the purity of his eyes shining on them??

His mental sufferings as he stands there probably cause him more anguish than the physical pains in his body. The injustice done to him: 'What wrong has he done?' Pilate asked the mob in the courtyard below. They trumped up one charge after another, each of which was found to be false.

Jesus turns his eyes from Pilate and looks down at the mob in the street below. A few days ago many of those now standing there were also in the procession into Jerusalem making the streets echo with a different cry – 'Hosanna', welcoming their leader. What a contrast in just a few days. He had wept on that Palm Sunday too, no doubt because he clearly saw and knew that they had missed the whole purpose of his coming. Who else is down there in the crowd? Yes, some who really love him, Mary his mother, Mary Magdalene and John. Nothing can ever separate them from him or him from them, although they don't realize that just yet.

What was running through his mind? He could have broken his enemies and torturers, he could have frozen their hearts with terror by throwing away his crown, instantly healing his wounds, casting off the purple robe and showing himself in all of his mighty glory. I wish he had! Why didn't he? He could have if he wanted to. What was the deep secret of his peace, stillness? All through this he is looking to and trusting the Father, whose face of beauty none but he has seen.

He is now moving on away from Pilate's house through the streets, people everywhere, some laughing and jeering others in a state of shock and weeping. Those who hate him, those who come out of curiosity and those who love him – which group would you have been in?

Sometimes a cross was set up permanently in the ground at the place of crucifixion, so the condemned man did not have to carry it. This did not happen for Jesus Christ despite his exhausted state. What must he have felt having to carry such a weight? The horizontal beam measured about six feet across, the longer beam was twice that length. It would have been difficult even for a big, healthy strong man to handle for the cross was not only heavy but too awkwardly shaped to be easily carried. The streets were narrow, and crowded with thousands of visitors who had come to see the 'show' and Jesus Christ still said nothing. A weak man? No way, this Jesus could not be broken.

There is a tradition that the soldiers tied his arms to the cross beam to make sure the cross would not slip. If this was the case he would not have the use of his hands to break a fall, but his face would strike the hard pavement. At one point along the route there is an incline reaching down rather steeply into a ravine. He falls down. Stop reading for a moment and just think. Jesus Christ lying there flat on his face with the

cross on his shoulders pressing him into the ground –
who is he and why is he there?

Jesus falls again, so Simon of Cyrene, someone Jesus
has never met before, carried the cross. Perhaps relieved
of the weight he can walk a little less painfully now.
Christ stops to speak to the weeping women, still in
control of the situation. He halts here because he wants
to halt. He speaks unhurriedly although he is well
aware of the impatience of his enemies. Quite firmly he
imposes a delay and they feel powerless to oppose him.
What does he say? 'Weep not over me but over
yourselves and your children . . .' When he has
finished they try to make up for lost time by urging him
forward all the more.

They arrive at Calvary. Jesus is stripped and then
tied to the cross before being nailed, otherwise the
nervous twitch would rip open his hands and feet. His
executioners stretch out each arm full along the trans-
verse beam, making both secure with several coils of
rope or cord. Then each leg is treated similarly. This
pain on top of all that he has suffered! He still doesn't
say anything.

The soldiers offer Jesus a drink, but 'when he had
tasted, he would not drink.' The drink might deaden
the pain, but he refuses it. Calvary is near a city gate
situated between two important roads, one going to
Joppa and the other to Damascus. People pass up and
down continually. They provoke him, 'Ha, Ha! You
boasted you could destroy God's temple and build it
again. . . . Now then, save yourself.' Even his two
fellow criminals join in the anger, though eventually
one turns humbly to Jesus. Throughout not a sugges-
tion of anger, not a single gesture of impatience, not a
syllable of complaint has come from him. Jesus is no

mere man. 'If I be lifted up from the earth', he said, 'I will draw all men to myself.'

Mary his mother stands and listens and looks. She hears the foul language of the soldiers, seated and playing dice, their job done, just filling in time till the three men die. She hears them bargaining over her son's robe and finally deciding to cast lots for it. What would she have given for the chance to have the robe herself and bring it home! Amongst all this she notes the marvellous silence of Jesus.

8: The Solution – Part 2

The last sermon

We read that men condemned to die on a cross often poured out a frightful volley of blasphemy and obscenity, calling down vengeance on those who had made them suffer. The soldiers took little notice of this at Calvary. It always happened. But what must have caused them astonishment was that Christ, all through his frightful tortures, had not murmured a word of complaint or shown the smallest sign of anger. In all their grim experience they had never before encountered a criminal who behaved like this one.

First Word: Father, forgive them, they know not what they do

He is silent as they hammer the nails into his hands and feet; silent as they stretch out his limbs on the cross; silent as it sinks with a thud into the ground and raised, increasing his agony. Now the cross is in position. Their job is done. They must now be wondering what he will say, as the other two are screaming and blaspheming. They sit and play a game and suddenly their attention is diverted. Jesus is saying something! 'Father', he says,

'forgive them, they do not know what they are doing.'
Those who hear are amazed, almost stunned, as if they
didn't quite hear it properly or were unconvinced by
what they heard. He repeats the first words several
times 'Father forgive them.' What kind of a man is he?
In agony, dying, yet forgiving those who had caused his
agony. This is why I believe in Jesus, and feel proud
about letting it be known publicly – because publicly he
forgave me, and publicly I received his forgiveness. I
am one of those who nailed him there. My sins
caused his pain. Someone once said that if I was the
only person in the world who had done wrong and
needed forgiving, he would have died for me. And he
did. He died for the world, but he also died for you and
for me, taking our punishment from God that we may
be totally forgiven. The old washed away! Not just a
new start in life, but a new life to start.

We often talk about Christ who died on the cross. He
also lived on the cross for three hours, using the cross
as a pulpit from which to deliver a sermon filled with
love. The entire sermon might have been preached in a
quarter of an hour. It contained, in all, only seven
sentences or 'words' but there was a pause after each.

This spacing out is deliberately planned. Jesus is
deeply concerned that we do not merely hear, but also
listen. These words are like seeds sown in us, which
must take root, so that, like Mary we may ponder over
them in our hearts, and they will grow, and may well
transform our lives. Otherwise they will blow away and
be forgotten.

Second Word: This day you shall be with me in paradise

One thief watches Jesus and witnesses in him unfaltering patience, which is more than just human. He hears him actually praying for the very persons who treated him so savagely. His own world has collapsed. Is it possible that Christ has the answer? Can he offer some hope? 'Lord,' he says, 'remember me when you come into your kingdom.' It is a poor compliment to Christ that the thief turns to him only when everything else has failed. But this is true of so many people. Would any of us treat a friend like this? He offers me his friendship and I reject it. I go my own way only to find that I too am unwanted where I go. Time passes and I continue to ignore him. Suppose, only after a lifetime, when there is no one else to fall back upon, I am finally willing to accept his friendship . . . how does he feel?! Yet Christ accepts the thief eagerly, even at this eleventh hour. The thief has made a modest enough request: 'Lord, remember me. . . .' Jesus responds with divine liberality. He promises not only a remembrance but, 'I solemnly promise you that this day you will be with me in paradise.' If regret at that moment were possible for the dying man, it would be in the thought that while he has indeed found Christ, he made the discovery *only now*.

At first this thief had joined with his companion in cursing Christ: '. . . the thieves who were crucified with him shouted . . . "If you are the son of God, save yourself and us".' To each, Christ offers unlimited grace and total forgiveness, but the unrepentant thief rejects it. The heart cannot be forced to love. Christ offers. Christ appeals. Christ promises. Christ warns and even threatens, but he forces no one. (God even waited for Mary to give her free consent to the incarnation). The unrepentant thief notices his companion change. For they *both* blasphemed against

Christ. Then one lapses into silence. When next he speaks, it is to pray to Christ and rebuke his companion. 'Have you no fear of God at all?' he asks, 'You got the same sentence as he did, but in our case we deserved it, we are paying for what we did, but this man has done no evil.'

Third word: Behold your son; behold your mother – A parting gift

There is a something in our nature that makes us value a parting gift from one who dies or goes away. Christ knows this. He is lying on his deathbed, the hard bed of the cross, with a crown of thorns as his pillow. He opens his eyes and looks at his mother Mary and his beloved disciple John. To Mary he says, 'Woman, behold your son,' and to John: 'Behold your mother'. A parting gift to each of great value. He has given his disciples a parting gift – the breaking of bread and drinking of wine in memory of his death. You cannot estimate the beauty and value of a gift until you take time to examine it. If it is a book you must read it. If it comes as a parcel in the mail you must remove the wrapping. And Jesus while on the cross says 'Behold,' learn to appreciate, still teaching his disciple John, and still remembering his mother, making sure she is cared for and comforted.

Fourth Word: My God, my God, why have you forsaken me?

It's December 23rd – a husband, kind and considerate and steady at his work, cycles five miles to get a few treats for the Christmas dinner. On his return he collapses and dies. The wife is totally forsaken and alone. Or the husband, due to arrive home from work to go off on the family holiday with his wife and three children, doesn't turn up. The wife has been busy all day, suitcases packed, children ready, no message, nothing. Three weeks later the police find that he's run away with another woman. The wife feels totally deserted. What must Jesus' experience really have been like? When he was insulted by men or ignored or contradicted, he always had one unfailing support to sustain him. He could always depend on the nearness of his heavenly Father. John's Gospel refers to the Father one hundred and sixteen times as being the source of strength and consolation to his Son, '. . . I am not alone, because the Father is with me . . .' But here at Calvary, even this one dependable support seems to give way.

'God gave his only son that whosoever believes in him should not perish but have everlasting life.' At this point all the sins of the world, everything you and I have ever done wrong was put on Jesus. Jesus was the sacrificed lamb and carried the burden and the punishment alone. The perfect Father cannot look on sin and turns from it and so Jesus the Son is utterly alone, bearing the load. What a great work he did.

Forsaken, desolate. How could we ever understand this experience? Jesus forsaken by God in order to restore us to that place in God's heart.

Fifth Word: I thirst

This word on the cross is the only direct reference he makes to his sufferings. 'I thirst.' Imagine, a sponge is lying on the ground, used perhaps by the soldiers to wipe the blood off their arms and hands. One of them steeps it in vinegar, places it on a stick about a foot long and holds it to the lips of the dying Christ. He sips a little from the sponge. Can you guess the intensity of the agony he suffered from this thirst? He had neither eaten nor drunk since the supper last night. He had lost a huge quantity of blood, especially in the scourging. His mouth is parched, his tongue so dry it sticks to his teeth and his lips are cut and swollen. 'No man ever spoke the way this man spoke', we are told. Words that comforted. Words that scorched. Words of beauty and depth. Now he can scarcely speak at all, yet he manages to croak, 'I thirst'. Is it because he has something else to say? Something to say to us and so needs to moisten his mouth a little to prepare his tongue for a word or words, or could it be a shout?

Sixth Word: It is finished

He shouts out 'TETELESTAI', meaning it is accomplished, it is fulfilled, it is done. 'It is finished' on the lips of Jesus is indeed a shout of victory, and he has won this battle, despite appearances. 'Where, O death, is your victory? Where, O death, is your sting?' He tells us, too, how to turn the *seeming* failure of Calvary into a magnificent success, summed up so well in the New Testament, 'For the message of the cross is foolishness to those who are perishing, but to those who are being saved it is the power of God. For it is written: 'I will destroy the wisdom of the wise; the intelligence of the intelligent I will frustrate'. Where is the wise man? Where is the scholar? Where is the philosopher of this age? Has not God made foolish the wisdom of the world? For since in the wisdom of God the world through its wisdom did not know him, God was pleased through the foolishness of what was preached to save those who believe. Jews demand miraculous signs and Greeks look for wisdom, but we preach Christ crucified, a stumbling block to Jews and foolishness to Gentiles, but to those whom God has called, both Jews and Greeks, Christ the power of God and the wisdom of God. For the foolishness of God is wiser than man's wisdom, and the weakness of God is stronger than man's strength' (1 Corinthians 1.18–25).

9: The Cross Interpreted

One of the most remarkable paintings I have ever seen is Salvador Dali's *Christ of St. John of the Cross* which hangs in the Glasgow Art Gallery. There is something very different about this painting compared with others of the crucifixion. The cross itself is massive and looms over the world. The figure on the cross is young and strong . . . and he seems to be holding back the great forces of darkness and evil, and in the foreground the earth, sea and sky are lit with a powerful new light streaming from the crucified figure. 1 John 2.8 says, 'the darkness is passing and the true light is already shining.'

The cross dominates the world and the world that the artist sees is the world on which Christ looks from his cross. And seeing the world from the angle of the cross brings in a new perspective. 1 Samuel 16.7 reads, 'God does not see as man sees.'

Looking straight at the cross is difficult. Difficult because the cross is a horrifying and graphic picture of violence, brutality and pain. It stands at the heart of all that is unpleasant and revolting. We can be outraged by the details of a real crime and yet be absolutely enthralled and captivated by the same details in a fictitious one. The Government endeavours to stop crime and our morality condemns it, yet many people's imagination feeds on it. Without the spilling of blood the drama is weak and there is no excitement. We respond to this sort of thing because somehow it is part of the stuff of life and also the horror of senseless and unnecessary violence somehow thrills. But the cross is real, it is not a fake story (and we know that!), and the real cross is a horrible sight. The cross of Jesus is a *true* story about pain, agony and heartbreak – things we like to avoid. The cross is also dangerous because of the effect it has on people when they really see it. It either brings out the best or the worst in people. It brought out the best in Mary Magdalene, the centurion, the disciple John who watched the nightmare scene. It brought out the worst in Herod, Pilate, Judas and the soldiers. It brought out the best in one thief and it brought out the worst in the other. This is what is meant by the cross judging us. It judges us because it assesses us and shows us up . . . showing up our true colours.

We have observed the journey to the cross and the seven unforgettable words from the cross in our last two chapters. In this chapter we want to understand its meaning and its significance, if any, to us. We want to try and take a look at things the way Salvador Dali tried to, looking from the cross at the world, rather than from the world looking at the cross. Problems of course do not vanish when looked at in the light of the cross, but often their contours change. People remain people but seen from the cross show up in a different light. Only from the cross was it possible to see both thieves as they really were. Jesus has a unique angle on all of us. Maybe we should just pause and pray, even if we have never prayed before, that if God *is* God and all this about the cross of Jesus did happen for us, to pray that he would . . . help us understand it.

Somebody (I can't remember who) once said, 'do not turn from the awful horror of the cross, or you will lose the solemn power of it'. That is so true because the cross will make us realists as nothing else can, realists about ourselves, others, the world and God. The cross makes short work of all illusions – and it begins with those illusions about ourselves.

The Cross Interpreted

The first group of Christians, known as the 'early Church', met with opposition and many challenges. The main challenge was to explain themselves! How did the early Church differ from the rest of the Jews? The Christians believed that the Messiah had come, that Jesus was the Christ, but the rest of the Jews did not believe this. Outwardly this seemed the only real difference between the two groups of Jews. The early Church had to answer questions. 'Why, if Jesus was the Christ, did he die or be executed?' For the Jews the idea of a crucified Christ was the real stumbling block. 1 Corinthians 1.23 explains,

'but we preach Christ crucified, a stumbling block to Jews and foolishness to Gentiles.'

It trips people up because it delivers a wound to human pride. There is nothing else that cuts us down to size as quickly as the cross. When we come seriously and consider the death of Jesus Christ our thoughts of pride and self-sufficiency are cut down to size. The Jews at the time of Jesus were very proud and especially so of their character. They had a tremendous zeal and passion for righteousness (doing right) and thought this could be achieved by obeying a complicated and often petty set of rules. The great mistake they made was to imagine that they succeeded. For the Jews a crucified Messiah went against their whole understanding and expectations and the whole idea seemed like a blasphemous joke! By their own understanding they arrived at the conclusion that the true Messiah would *immediately* liberate them from bondage to a foreign power – if there were to be any crucifixions it would be Romans who would be on the crosses and Jews who would put them there. This was the atmosphere surrounding the early Church.

So the Jews' questions had to be answered. There were two main problems, first 'Why did Jesus die?' and then, 'What did his death achieve?' These two same questions, two thousand years later, still remain the basic questions about the cross.

Why did Jesus die?

This needs to be answered on two levels, first on a historical level and secondly on a 'theological' level. The first and obvious reason for Jesus' death was of course that some of his contemporaries simply did not like him. Taking into account the Jews and their ideas of righteousness and all that, you can imagine their response when the carpenter from Nazareth came preaching that they should repent (turn away from their sins), telling them that they were lost, that judgement was coming, and that there was no hope for them, except the forgiveness, new life and hope that he was offering. Some of the Jews' reaction was, 'Who does this ignorant person think he is?', 'How dare he come into our world disturbing, interrupting and interfering?' And indeed that's what he did, he upset the ecclesiastics (the religious people . . . who hadn't really understood it) because he criticized them and the Church of his day – note that even the so-called 'people of God' were not beyond criticism! So they decided that his career must be brought to a swift end. But God is a critic – this is the meaning of judgement – and never more so than of his own people. All judgement begins at the house of God. We find this to be true today. There are those who call themselves Christians and are members of a church, but are self-sufficient and uninvolved. Some may be sincere and go to church, or if they don't actually attend, they patronize it, 'It's a good thing you know . . . church that is . . . but for the very young and very old!' The same people think they have a first class ticket to heaven under their pillows . . . and boy, those citizens of heaven are going to be mighty fortunate to have them in their company. That's human pride . . . and that doesn't send you to heaven! So his contemporaries were in on it. But the State also had its say in the death of Jesus.

Caesar was ruler and obviously exercised power. Jesus acknowledged the place and the rights of the State and made reference to our duties to it. He also recognized the role of the State in history and took it very seriously. But despite all this he still set limits to the claims of the State . . . *It is not divine*, as some would want to think, as has been shown in every period of history from Nebuchadnezzar and Augustus to Hitler and Stalin. E. Stauffer in his book *Christ and the Caesars* summed it up like this:

The history of man is the history of guilt rolling through the ages like an ever-increasing avalanche.

This guilt resulted from self-glorification, which shattered first the community between man and God and then, the community between man and man. From that time every historical community has been merely an emergency structure on a shattered foundation.'

All this may sound and seem distant from the trial and death of Jesus, but in fact it is not. The reason why the State in the person of Pilate representing Caesar agreed without protest to the condemnation of Jesus was that he posed a political threat. He had spoken about a kingdom, his kingdom, different from the empire of Rome, and with another King, different from the person of Caesar! In fact, within only a few generations from this time the Church was persecuted on the grounds that it was a threat to the Empire. But had they understood Jesus' teaching, they would have realized that he was never a threat to the Empire as such. Jesus himself had said, 'My kingdom is not of this world.' Even so, Jesus did challenge any idea of the State claiming man's total allegiance especially the idea that the Emperor is in place of God! This conflict was present when Pilate and Jesus met and these were the decisive issues in the trial of Jesus when Pilate senﻬnced him to death.

But the people also had their say. The trial of Jesus was not completely undemocratic even though it was conducted in an undemocratic fashion! It was the crowd, who shouted out, 'Crucify, crucify him'. This time the crowd was indeed powerful, and for once they got what they wanted. The criticisms Jesus had spoken threatened the Church, the kingdom of Jesus had threatened the State, but the morality of Jesus threatened the people.

We certainly don't always like having our morals questioned and as to having them exposed, that's usually out of the question. But the life of Jesus showed up the deeds of men in the dazzling light of his sheer goodness. It demanded and compelled a decision, a choice. People could either repent and ask for forgiveness like many did *or* reject him and shout out 'Crucify him'. Either repentance or resentment! Despite the fact that we agree with our hearts in goodness, a 'good' man makes us uncomfortable and we would rather view him at a distance. It may be a little embarrassing to be shown up in his light; how much more embarrassing must it have been when God walked the streets? In Jesus, God had come a bit too near for some. So Jesus must die, and die he did.

To leave the answer to the question, 'Why did Jesus die?' on this level would be to over-simplify it. Death did not take Jesus by surprise. Many times throughout his three-year public ministry Jesus made references to his death. At Caesarea Philippi when Simon Peter understood for the first time who Jesus was, there followed from Jesus a series of three sayings about the suffering, the death and the resurrection of the Son of Man, the third of which was quite detailed.

'We are going up to Jerusalem,' he said, 'and the Son of Man will be betrayed to the chief priests and teachers of the law. They will condemn him to death and will hand him over to the Gentiles, who will mock him and spit on him, flog him and kill him. Three days later he will rise' (Mark 10.33).

Jesus knew very well what was before him and what his destiny would be (in detail as this passage from the Bible reveals!). He also knew that God's purposes would all be fulfilled through men even through their crimes. Therefore the cross was no unforeseen accident, taking him by surprise.

This was also a key point in the preaching of the first disciples. They answered the question, 'Why did Jesus die?' on two levels. Firstly, without any thought of embarrassment they laid the reponsibility and guilt at the door of the people themselves – the actual audience they were addressing, and on themselves as well. And they certainly didn't hesitate to press this home:

'The God of our fathers raised Jesus from the dead – whom you had killed by hanging him on a tree.'
(Acts 5.30)

But they also saw God's plan in it all:

'This man was handed over to you by God's set purpose and foreknowledge, and you, with the help of wicked men, put him to death by nailing him to the cross.'   (Acts 2.23)

Jesus accepted the cross as the will of God for him but right up to the evening of Gethsemane he seems to have hoped and prayed that there might be some other way. Nevertheless the cross happened because there just was no other way.

I am constantly amazed but not surprised by the way that God's purpose is often accomplished and fulfilled through events which he can hardly be said to have caused. For example he did not cause Caiaphas to seek the death of Jesus, nor Judas to betray him, nor Pilate to condemn him, but took these evil choices and wove them into his purpose. The theological reason therefore for the death of Jesus was the fulfilment of God's purpose. Jesus went through with it all because there was no other way that the sins of the world could be dealt with. In the words of a hymn:

> There was no other good enough
> To pay the price of sin
> He only could unlock the gate
> Of heaven, and let us in.

Which leads to the second question . . .

What did his death achieve?

The cross achieved forgiveness, victory over evil powers, a radical dealing with sin, a final conquest of death —and yet still more! Still more because the meaning of the cross can never be exhausted by Christian thought. But the things that are clear about the cross are very clear. First God speaks, secondly God acts, thirdly God enters into personal relationships with people and fourthly, God makes men good.

1. God speaks

The cross speaks a word about man and a word about God. As far as man is concerned the word is sinful. In the cross we see the ultimate meaning of all our sin. It is anti-God and causes God pain. So God has to deal with sin. And the death of his Son on the cross is what it actually cost God to deal with it. Yet through it all we see in the cross of Jesus, the love of God.

> God demonstrates his own love for us in this:
> while we were still sinners, Christ died for us.
>
> (Romans 5.8)

In the cross God has spoken, through the cross we may know what he is like and experience his love for each one of us.

2. God acts

On the cross, God was *doing* as well as *saying*. He was in fact doing what he was saying. If we sum it up in one word, it is 'rescue'. God's action in the cross is a rescuing one, reaching down to the deepest point of every man's need. The biblical word used for rescue is redemption and in Romans 3.24 the Apostle Paul puts it like this, '. . . justified freely by his grace through the redemption that came by Christ Jesus.' In the minds of Paul's original readers the idea of a redeemer would conjure up a picture of a great benefactor freeing prisoners or slaves by actually paying some ransom price for them. This, the apostle Paul says, is what Jesus Christ has done for men through the cross. He has set them free from bondage to sin.

The word redemption is also associated in the Bible with blood. The death of Jesus is a murder story! And in this story blood is a necessity, there is no other way; Hebrews 9.22 says, 'Without the shedding of blood there is no forgiveness.' So the blood in this story is not to add to the drama, because its actual shedding has some permanent effect on the moral situation of the universe. It deals with the problem of human sin. But only Jesus' blood could do this because only Jesus is perfect. So within one crime against Jesus is the final conquest of all crime. Because of one victim, there is the hope of release and pardon for all criminals. The teaching of the New Testament about the blood of Christ is nothing less than this. But the act of redemption was also an act of sacrifice. Jesus actually offered *himself* as a sacrifice. And through this sacrifice God forgives sinners and deals with their sin and gets rid of it. It's only when God really deals with sin that forgiveness can be real, because we cannot live with God so long as our guilt is not cleared. We cannot simply become good friends once more, because God's anger against our sin is not just a passing mood but is a permanent dividing force. So the cross is God's way in which the strength of his love breaks through the reality of his anger. The cross therefore marks God's decision within history to rescue us!

3. *God enters into personal relationships with people*
The cross is the decisive movement of God towards the people he loves – you and me. The cross is love transformed to meet the needs of a particular and desperate situation. The cross is the reunion of that which was separated. The New Testament word for this is reconciliation. The cross enabled God and man to meet on new terms. Sin had caused an estrangement. God and man had, as it were, lost each other. But through the cross entirely new relationships have now become possible between man and God and consequently between man and man. They can be reconciled.

The initiative in the matter was taken by God, we are at the receiving end. We could not have accomplished our own reconciliation with God but we can refuse it. So the cross brings men into new personal relations with God. God and man, the holy and the sinful, can meet in the *one* place, Calvary, through the one mediator Jesus Christ. It is there that the new relations begin.

Meeting God at the cross of Jesus Christ leads to peace with God, 'making peace through his blood, shed on the cross' (Colossians 1.20). There need no longer be feelings of hostility with self, others and God. It leads a person into a new freedom, he is 'made free from sin' (Romans 6.18). He is able to overcome temptation to sin and he no longer lives under a sense of failure or frustration or condemnation. Above all, when he experiences reconciliation he is given the privileges of sonship to God. He can begin to experience the joy of being in God's family, and calling God Father, and the privilege of working for and serving him. Standing within this new relationship and enjoying this new liberty the Christian can begin to become the person God meant him to be. It is the cross that makes this possible!

4. *God makes men good*

Out of this new relationship moral progress and transformation come. There will be no sudden leap into goodness but the result of being forgiven will give you power to look at yourself and what you are like and what you have done straight in the face. Such acceptance of the facts and the situation of your life is the foundation of all healing. We begin by being forgiven and all that this implies, and from that point *he* can begin (if you let him) to make you good. C.S. Lewis described the Christian life as 'going in for the full treatment'. Turning from sins and asking Christ's forgiveness gives you the privilege of receiving his Holy Spirit. Jesus after his resurrection went to heaven because if he stayed on earth in his bodily human form he could only have been at one place at any one time so we could not all talk to him. He promised that after he returned to heaven, God would send the Holy Spirit into the world, and that the Spirit would dwell within every Christian. The Bible teaches that the Holy Spirit is like an interpreter, revealing Christ, illuminating his teaching, and making his cross real.

A former Archbishop of Canterbury, Michael Ramsey, expressed it all in a way I like, because the Christian life is in no way easy but worth it!

> 'Not only did the crucifixion make possible the giving of the Spirit, but the life bestowed by the Spirit is a life of which crucifixion is a quality, a life of living through dying.'

Jesus died for you and for me. We have looked at the way he died, why he died and what he died for. And yet after reading these chapters it may still seem a mystery (I'm not surprised!). Let the cross be a mystery to the mind; intellectual humility in the face of God will do none of us any harm. But there is no doubt that the cross is full of meaning for daily living and relevant for all who are consciously sinful and consciously guilty and consciously in a mess (do you know anyone not included in this bracket?). The cross touches life at its point of felt need. So let the cross be a mystery not because of itself but because of him who died on it and what he did on it. The real mystery of course is the crucified!

10: Resurrected

In the history of the world, only one tomb has ever had a rock rolled in front of it, and a soldier guard set to watch it to prevent the dead man within from escaping: that was the tomb of Jesus Christ on the evening of the Friday we now call Good Friday. What sight could be more ridiculous than armed soldiers keeping their eyes on a corpse? They said he was dead, they knew he was dead, they said he would not rise again and yet they watched suspiciously! They remembered that he called his body the Temple and said that in three days after they destroyed it, he would rebuild it. They recalled too, that he compared himself to Jonah and said that as Jonah was in the belly of the whale for three days, so would he be in the belly of the earth for three days and then would rise again. Jesus was dead – what would happen on the third day? Early Saturday morning therefore the chief priests and the Pharisees broke the Sabbath law and presented themselves to Pilate saying:

'Sir, we remember that while that liar was still alive
he said, I will be raised to life three days later.
Give orders, then for his tomb to be carefully
guarded until the third day, so that his disciples
will not be able to go and steal the body, and then

tell the people that he was raised from death. This
last lie would be even worse than the first one.

(Matthew 27.63–64)

Their request for a guard until the 'third day' had
more reference to Christ's words about his resurrection
than it did to the fear of the disciples stealing a corpse
and propping it up like a living thing! Pilate however
was in no mood to discuss this with them, for they were
the reason why he had condemned innocent blood. He
had made his own official investigation that Christ was
dead so Pilate said to them:

'You may have your guard, go and make it secure
as best you can.'   (Matthew 27.65)

I wonder what went through the mind of Pilate as he
was saying those words, 'as best you can,' for if Jesus of
Nazareth was going to rise nothing was going to stop
him. . . . 'Maybe', thought Pilate.

'So they went and made the grave secure, they
sealed the stone and left the guard in charge.'

(Matthew 27.66)

The most astounding fact about this was that the
enemies of Christ seemed to expect the resurrection,
but his friends did not. It was the believers who were
the sceptics. It was the unbelievers who were credu-
lous. His followers needed and demanded proofs
before they would be convinced. In the great scenes
of the resurrection told in the Bible there is a note of
sadness and unbelief. The first scene is that of a
weeping Mary Magdalene who came to the grave

early in the morning with spices, not to greet the risen saviour, but to anoint his dead body. . . .

Early Sunday morning several women went to the tomb. The very fact that the women brought spices proved tht they did not expect a resurrection. It seems so strange that they all thought this way, especially as Jesus made many references to the fact that he would rise from the dead. . . . It just did not occur to them that Jesus' resurrection could be possible. When the stone was rolled to the door of the tomb, not only was Christ buried but also all of their hopes. How interesting that so many people assume that the followers of Jesus easily believed! They found it as hard to believe as perhaps we do. The only thought the women had was to anoint the body of the dead Christ. Joseph of Arimathea and Nicodemus had heaped a generous quantity of spices over Jesus' body, but the women wanted to add their bit as well. How they were to get into the tomb appears not to have entered their minds until they were approaching it. When the women came near they saw that the stone, great as it was, had been rolled away already. But they did not jump to the conclusion that his body had risen. Instead of the dead body of Jesus, they saw an angel.

'Don't be alarmed', he said, 'I know you are looking for Jesus of Nazareth, who was crucified. He is not here – he has been raised! Look, here is the place where they put him. Now go and give this message to his disciples, including Peter: He is going to Galilee ahead of you; there you will see him, just as he told you.'   (Mark 16.6–7)

Tombstones often bear the inscription, 'Here lies . . .'. Then follows the name of the dead and perhaps some praise of the one departed. But here in contrast, the angel did not write, but expressed a very different epitaph: 'He is not here.'

So they went and told the disciples, not that Jesus had risen from the dead but that 'They have taken the Lord out of his tomb, and we do not know where they have laid him' (John 20.2). Peter and John ran to the tomb to find only the linen cloths which were used to wrap the body of Jesus inside the tomb. (If anyone had stolen the body, would they in their haste have bothered to unwrap it and left the linen cloths?) The Bible says 'Until then they (Peter and John) had not understood the scriptures, which showed that he must rise from the dead' (John 20.9). They had the facts and the evidence of the resurrection, but they did not yet understand its full meaning. Jesus then began the first of his eleven appearances between his resurrection and ascension. The first of these was to Mary Magdalene who returned to the tomb after Peter and John had left it.

Finding the tomb still empty she burst into tears. With her eyes still brimming, she vaguely saw someone near her who asked, 'Why are you weeping?' she said 'They have taken my Lord away, and I do not know where they have put him' (John 20.13–14). When she had said this, she turned and saw Jesus standing there but she did not know that it was Jesus – she thought he was the gardener – the gardener of Joseph of Arimathea to whom the tomb belonged. Believing this man might know where the body of Jesus could be found, Mary Magdalene went down on her knees and asked, 'If you took him away, sir, tell me where you

have put him, and I will go and get him' (John 20.15).
Poor Mary, worn out since Good Friday, with no
strength left yet eager to 'take him away'. Jesus said to
her, 'Mary'. That voice was more startling than a clap
of thunder. She turned casting herself at his feet and
grasping them. She could only say, 'Rabboni', which is
the Hebrew word for Master, Teacher.

After many hours of darkness there was new light,
after many hours of hopelessness, this hope, after the
search this discovery. Mary was always at his feet. It
was there she first anointed him. She was there as she
stood at the cross. Now, in joy at seeing the Master,
she threw herself at his feet to embrace them. Jesus
said to her 'Do not hold on to me, because I have not
yet gone back up to the Father. But go to my brothers
and tell them that I am returning to him who is my
Father and their Father, my God and their God (John
20.17). Her tears, he suggested, were to be dried not
because she had seen him again, but because he was the
Lord of life. When he had ascended to the Father, then
he would send the Spirit of truth, who would be their
new comforter and his inner presence – then she would
know him the truly risen glorified Christ.

This was his first hint, after his resurrection, at the
new relationship he would have with men, of which he
spoke so clearly the night of the Last Supper. This
was the first time he ever called his disciples 'brothers' –
a new relationship with God. It took the crucifixion
to make it possible for others to be called sons of
God. But there would be a vast difference between
himself as the natural son and human beings, who
through his Spirit would become the adopted sons.
That's why he made a distinction between 'my Father'
and 'their Father'. Never once in his life did he say

'our Father' as if the relationship were the same between God and himself and others. Sonship was by nature his, only by grace and adoption are we able to become sons of God. So Jesus did not tell Mary to inform the disciples just that he was risen but rather that he would ascend. His purpose was not just to stress that he who had died was now alive, but that this was the beginning of a spiritual kingdom which would become visible when he sent his Spirit.

So Mary rushed quickly to tell the disciples what Jesus had said. Did they believe her? Not in the least! Scepticism, doubt and unbelief, they thought that what Mary was saying was just nonsense. This was a forecast of the way the world would receive the news of Jesus' death and resurrection. Mary Magdalene and the other women did not at first believe in the resurrection, they had to be convinced. Neither did the disciples believe. Their response was 'You know women! Always imagining things.' What modern sceptics say about the resurrection story, the disciples themselves were the first to say, namely, it was an idle tale. The disciples dismissed the whole story as a delusion. You could not convince them. When Mohammed died, Omar rushed from his tent, sword in hand and declared that he would kill anyone who said that the Prophet had died. In the case of Christ there was a readiness to believe that he had died, but a reluctance to believe that he was living.

Meanwhile, after Mary had gone to tell the disciples, the guards went to tell the chief priests what had happened. 'The chief priests met with the elders and made their plan; they gave a large sum of money to the soldiers and said you are to say that his disciples came during the night and stole his body while you were asleep' (Matthew 28.12).

The bribery of the guard was really a stupid way to escape the fact of the resurrection. While it was very unlikely that a whole guard of Roman soldiers had fallen asleep while they were on duty, it was even more absurd for them to say what had happened while they were asleep. Quite apart from the fact that the soldiers were advised to say that they were asleep and yet so awake as to have seen thieves and to know that they were Jesus' disciples, it is equally improbable that a few timid disciples should attempt to steal their Master's body from a grave closed by stone, officially sealed and guarded by soldiers, without awakening the sleeping guards! The removal of the body would have been to no purpose so far as the disciples were concerned, nor had any of them even thought of it!

On that same Easter Sunday Jesus made another appearance to two of his followers who were on their way to a village named Emmaus which was a short distance from Jerusalem. It was not so long before that their hopes had been burning brightly, but the darkness of Good Friday and the burial in the tomb caused them to lose all their gladness. No subject was more in people's minds that particular day than the person of Christ and the sadness of his death. As they were busy discussing the events of the past few days, a 'stranger' drew near to them. It was the risen Jesus Christ, but, like Mary Magdalene, they failed to recognize him. Jesus asked, 'What is it you are talking about to each other, as you walk along?' (Luke 24.17). They halted, their faces full of gloom! Obviously, the reason these two followers of Jesus were sad was because of their bereavement. One of the two, whose name was Cleopas, was the first to speak. He expressed amazement at the ignorance of the stranger who was apparently so unfamiliar with the events of the last few days. 'Are you the only person staying in Jerusalem not to know what has happened there in the last few days?' (Luke 24.18). Jesus asked 'What do you mean?' The whole story came tumbling from their lips. The disciples and followers of Jesus had been thinking of their leader as the one who, powerful in word and deed, would liberate Israel from Roman tyranny and oppression. But the unthinkable had happened: 'our chief priests and rulers delivered him up . . . and crucified him.' That was three days before and there were rumours that some women had found Jesus' tomb empty.

Jesus said, 'How foolish you are, how slow you are to believe everything the prophets said' (Luke 24.25). They were accused of being foolish and slow of heart because if they had ever sat down and examined what the prophets had said about the Messiah, they would have believed! The cross was the condition of glory. It was a necessity. So Jesus explained to them 'beginning with Moses and all the prophets, the passages which referred to Himself in every part of the Scriptures' (Luke 24.27).

Quoting from Isaiah – he showed the manner of his death and his last words from the cross.

Quoting from Daniel – how he was to become the mountain that filled the earth.

Quoting from Genesis – how the seed of a woman would crush the serpent of evil in human hearts.

Quoting from Moses – how he would be the brazen serpent that would be lifted up to heal men of evil.

Quoting from Isaiah – how he would be Emmanuel, God with us, and from many other scriptures he gave them the key to the mystery of God's life among men and the purpose of his coming. Like so many people today, the Emmaus-bound travellers had not understood the Old Testament, and so had completely misunderstood 'all that had happened in Jerusalem.'

At last they arrived at Emmaus and they begged him to stay with them. They had learned much, but they knew that they had not learned all. They still did not recognize him but there was a light about him. He accepted their invitation to be a guest. They immediately got supper ready and asked him to give thanks, 'He sat down to eat with them, took the bread and said the blessing, then he broke the bread and gave it to them. Then their eyes were opened and they recognized him but he disappeared from their sight' (Luke 24.30). Turning to one another they reflected, 'Did we not feel our hearts on fire as he talked with us on the road and explained the Scriptures to us?' (Luke 24.32). His influence on them was both effective and intellectual. Effective in the sense that it made their hearts burn and intellectual inasmuch as he gave them an understanding of the hundreds of pre-announcements of his coming, his death and his resurrection.

The two followers of Jesus returned immediately to Jerusalem to find the disciples in varying degrees of unbelief. The place where the disciples were that Easter Sunday evening was the upper room, where Jesus had met with them for the Last Supper only seventy-two hours before. Though the doors were shut, suddenly in the midst of them appeared the risen Jesus, greeting them with the words: 'Peace be with you'.

The disciples thought that they were seeing things. His presence, they thought could be accounted for in no natural way, since the doors were closed. Jesus said to them, 'Why are you alarmed? Why are these doubts coming up in your minds?' (Luke 24.38).

He showed them his hands and his feet which had been pierced with nails on the cross, then his side which had been speared open, saying to them: 'Look at my hands and my feet and see that it is I myself. Feel me and you will know' (Luke 24.39).

One of the disciples, probably John, moved forward and touched him for later on he wrote:

'It was there from the beginning, we have heard it, we have seen it with our own eyes. We looked upon it and felt it with our own hands.' (1 John 1.1)

John too would remember it when he wrote his Apocalypse (the book of Revelation) where he described the humanity of Jesus enthroned and adored in heaven: 'A lamb with the marks of slaughter upon him?' (Revelation 5.6).

So he would be recognized as one crucified though now in glory. These nail prints, this pierced side, these were the unmistakable scars of battle against sin and evil. But 'they still could not believe, they were so full of joy and wonder, so he asked them, 'Have you anything here to eat?' (Luke 24.41). They placed before him a piece of fish which he took and ate in their presence. *Then they believed*! This belief now gave them joy, but the joy was so great they could hardly believe it! At first they were too frightened to believe, now they were too joyful to believe. Jesus eating with them seemed to be the strongest proof to them of his resurrection.

After proving to his disciples that he had risen by showing them his hands, feet and side, and by eating before them, he said to them, 'Peace be with you, as the Father sent me, so I send you.'

Then Jesus breathed on them and gave them his Holy Spirit. It was but a cloud that would precede heavy rain. It was the breath of the Holy Spirit, a foretaste of the rushing wind of Pentecost (Acts 2). As in the beginning he had breathed into Adam the breath of natural life, so now he breathed into his disciples the breath of spiritual life, the foundation of his Church. As he breathed on them, he gave them the Holy Spirit, which marked them as his Sons.

On one occasion when Jesus was at a Temple festival, he got up on the last day of the celebrations and said, 'Whoever is thirsty should come to me and drink. As the Scripture says, whoever believes in me, streams of life-giving water will pour out from his heart.' Jesus said this about the Spirit, which those who believed in him were going to receive.

At that feast, he affirmed that he would first have to die and pass into glory, before the Holy Spirit could come. His words now implied that he was already in his state of glory, for he was giving them the Spirit. His Spirit is given to those who want to become Christians, his disciples, his followers, to give assurance that we are forgiven, to give us new life within and to enable us to become the people we are really meant to be.

Life means what? Life means encountering the resurrected Jesus Christ, putting the past behind, receiving grace for today and a hope to come, all and only through Jesus Christ. Life means knowing him. Maybe you are still unconvinced. I have left one person out of the resurrection story so far. Maybe you are just like him.

The first appearance of Jesus in the Upper Room was to only ten disciples. Judas was not there because he had committed suicide after betraying Jesus, but Thomas was not present. The reason for his absence is unknown. In three different passages of the Gospel, Thomas is always portrayed as looking on the pessimistic side of things, as regards both the present and the future. Immediately after the disciples became convinced of the resurrection, they told Thomas on his return. Thomas did not say he refused to believe, but that he was unable to believe until he had some tangible proof of the resurrection. This was in spite of the testimony of the ten other disciples that they had seen the risen Jesus!

'Unless I see the scars of the nails in his hands and put my finger on those scars and my hand in his side, I will not believe.' (John 20.25)

His refusal to trust the testimony of ten companions, who had seen the risen Jesus with their own eyes, proved how sceptical he was – how hard he found it to believe. This carried on for a week and then, the doors still closed, the risen Jesus walked in again and said, 'Peace be with you' (John 20.26).

Jesus spoke directly to Thomas, 'Put your finger here, and look at my hands, then stretch out your hand and put it in my side. Stop your doubting and believe!' (John 20.27). Jesus rebuked Thomas, 'Stop doubting', telling him to believe and shake off his gloom! Thomas was so convinced by positive proof that he fell to his knees and said to Jesus, 'My Lord and my God!' (John 20.28).

It was an acknowledgement that the Emmanuel of the Old Testament was before him. He, who was the last to believe, was the first to make the full confession of the divinity of the risen Jesus Christ. However, Jesus said to Thomas,

> 'Do you believe because you see me? How happy are those who believe without seeing me!'
>
> (John 20.29)

There are some who will not believe even when they see, such as Pharaoh in the Old Testament, others believe only when they see. Above both these types Jesus placed those who had not seen and yet believed. If Thomas had believed through the testimony of his fellow disciples, his faith in Christ would have been greater, for Thomas had often heard Jesus say that he would be crucified and rise again. He also knew from the Old Testament that the crucifixion was the fulfilment of a prophecy, but he wanted the additional proof of the senses.

Thomas thought that he was doing the right thing in demanding the full evidence of sensible proof, but what would become of future generations if the same evidence was to be demanded by them? The future believers Jesus implied, must accept the fact of the resurrection from those who had been with him. Jesus therefore says that you can believe without seeing and fully understand the mystery of the cross of Jesus Christ. Some credit must however be given to Thomas, who touched Christ as man, and believed in him as God.

Jesus' life was a struggle, but without the cross there could not be an empty tomb, without the crown of thorns, there would never have been a halo of light, unless there had been a Good Friday, there would not have been an Easter Sunday. Christianity is hard but great! When Jesus said 'I have conquered the world,' he did not mean his followers would be immune from pain, sorrow and crucifixion. What the resurrection offered was not immunity from evil in the physical world, but immunity from sin in the soul. Jesus did *not* tell his disciples, 'Be good and you will not suffer' but he did say, 'In this world you shall have tribulation.' He told them also not to fear those that kill the body. He told the disciples that his life was a model for all of his followers. Following Jesus and living out the Christian life is indeed not easy, but it's worth it, becoming a Christian you immediately receive a glimmer of heaven, of things to come.

Jesus' resurrection is the heart of Christianity. The resurrection validated everything Jesus said before and made sense of his death. It is not a belief that developed gradually, nor an emotional experience, but an actual event. Jesus Christ has the answers concerning life and death. He accepts us more than any person can, and through the cross he has overcome death, so we need not fear that. He is alive now, what will you do with him is the big question.

Life means what? 'We know also that the Son of God has come and has given us understanding, so that we may know him who is true. And we are in him who is true – even in his Son Jesus Christ. He is the true God and eternal life' (1 John 5.20).

11: Decision

Reading about Jesus and hearing his words one cannot simply close the book on him and forget. One chooses. Some prefer not to follow Jesus Christ. Deciding *not* to follow Jesus is saying 'no' to his forgiveness. Saying no to a cleansing of all the guilt in your life. Saying no to his love. Saying no to his Holy Spirit entering you and making you into the person you are meant to be. Saying no to working for him and being with him. Saying no to heaven. Saying no is your right. God will not force you.

But maybe you are saying 'yes' to these things. Maybe you are anxious to meet Jesus Christ. There is a story in the Bible about a man called Zacchaeus who was desperately anxious to meet Christ. In his desire to see Christ he was faced with difficulties amongst a crowd – he was a small man, and for this reason he had to find a way of catching Jesus' eye. His solution was to climb a tree, and risk becoming an object of laughter. Are we not *all* small, hidden in a crowd and prevented from seeing? The cost of seeing Jesus face to face for Zacchaeus was mockery. It seems that mockery is generally what stops more people than anything else in their quest for God. To be harshly criticized, attacked head on, to be disliked and rejected. All this goes against our pride, which wants to stand up to all that. It is not just a case of meeting Jesus, but meeting him and walking into him in the face of opposition. Jesus' way is a hard way and he made it very clear that he expected those who decided to follow him had to be prepared for action. People do not easily take on difficult tasks unless these involve the possibility of success and great rewards. When a leader inspires confidence, then difficulties if they arise can be faced and coped with. During the last World War, Churchill told his countrymen, 'I have nothing to offer you but blood, toil, tears and sweat.' Magnificent words that became a rallying cry, offsetting fear and despair and sparking a great positive effort against a human enemy that led ultimately to victory. Jesus was involved in a much more fearful struggle against the father of lies, the devil, and the enemy within every man the sinful self. The victory target in this case was a victory over sin and death, the prize to be won was freedom, truth and life.

The Bible quotes Jesus as saying, 'the gate may be narrow and the way very hard', but the struggle becomes a high adventure calling for great personal effort. When Jesus worked his miracles, he gave his followers something to do also. The disciples had to haul in the net filled with fish and on another occasion, distributed the loaves and fishes he had multiplied to thousands of people. Jesus was not a one-man show. His followers were active participants in his work. It is not easy to follow in the footsteps of Jesus, the road is hard and narrow and many turn from it, but for those that do the joy of sharing in his work is inexpressible!

Going back to the story about Zacchaeus. Jesus saw that Zacchaeus wanted to meet Jesus, so Jesus went to Zacchaeus' house to meet him personally. Jesus was received with reverence and joy – this joy had come about because of Zacchaeus' true conversion, which resulted after his act of repentance. A completely new direction for his life. Because of the peace Zacchaeus discovered with God through Jesus, he forgot the past. He was ready to right all wrongs and was anxious to start a new life free from the past. Jesus said to him, 'Today salvation has come to this house.' Do you want him to come to yours?

Why not take this step of commitment now? Say simply in your own words to Jesus something like this:

'Jesus, I come to you now, I have done many things wrong and I am guilty. I believe you died to set me free from this guilt. Thank you for dying for me. I believe you are alive and I am sorry for not letting you into my life before. I turn from all that is wrong, please come into my life now, and cleanse me and fill me with your Holy Spirit and start making me what I am meant to be. Thank you that I can now call you Lord. Thank you.'

If you have prayed this prayer, God has heard you and you have become a Christian. Christ has heard you and forgiven you and has entered your life by his Holy Spirit. Becoming a Christian is just like a marriage, it is commitment for life, but although it only takes a moment in committing oneself to a partner in marriage (like the prayer above), it can take a while getting adjusted.

An important question at this moment is of course, how do you know that in fact you are a Christian and that his Holy Spirit has come into your life as you invited him to?

Just as with the wedding couple, a promise was made. In the Bible we have God's promises. In Revelation 3.20 Jesus says, 'Here I stand knocking at the door. If anyone hears my voice and opens the door, I will come in.' It's a promise. The reason I have remained a Christian is because I can say that his promises have worked out in my life. In the Old Testament in the book of Numbers it says, 'God is not like men, who lie, he is not a human who changes his mind. Whatever he promises, he does, he speaks and it is done.' Be confident that he has done what he has promised. Faith is trusting someone's word. Christ is *trustworthy*. Trust him even if you don't feel like it. The new husband and wife may not feel much about their new marriage if they get dysentery on their honeymoon, but they're still married!

Starting and stopping makes no smooth progress and we must move on. So take some more steps. First there is the Bible. Read it. The first step in understanding the Bible is to begin to read it. Start with, say, John's Gospel and ask the Holy Spirit to help you understand what you read. Mark the verses that God speaks to you by and try to understand it in the light of the context in which it is set. Be determined and disciplined.

Secondly, there is prayer. Prayer is a means of developing your relationship with God, talking to him and listening to him. Start by thanking him. 'The Lord is great and is to be highly praised.' We can start by thanking God for Jesus, for food, home and friends, the things that happen during the day. If we fail and do wrong we can confess to him. 'If we confess our sins to God, He will keep his promise and do what is right, he will forgive us our sins and purify us from all our wrongdoing' (1 John 1.9). Learn to admit your faults and to claim the promise. Prayer is important in all its aspects and as someone once said, 'While it is obviously true that prayer affects the rest of your life, it is equally true that the rest of your life affects your prayer.' So make time to talk to him and tell him exactly what you think and feel. There is an enemy, Satan, and one of the things he would love to do is to stop our praying because he knows that if he can block our praying he can ruin our effectiveness. Someone once said:

'Satan laughs at the words we say,
Smiles at our efforts from day to day.
But he trembles when he sees
The weakest saint upon his knees.'

Thirdly, go to church. Find a church that firmly believes in the truths of Jesus Christ. When you commit yourself to Jesus Christ in personal allegiance, you join a world-wide family of others who have done the same thing. Therefore being with other Christians to learn and to receive teaching and encouragement is important. And fourthly, don't be ashamed to tell others about Jesus.

You will find that he blesses you for it and of course if Jesus is *truth*, there is nothing to be embarrassed about. Read your Bible, pray, go to church and confess him in your conversation. Take those next steps and see whether he will *not* shower his abundant glorious riches of heaven on you!

'Until we all reach unity in the faith and in the knowledge of the Son of God and become mature, attaining to the whole measure of the fullness of Christ.' (Ephesians 4.13)

If you wish to receive *regular information* about *new books*, please send your name and address to:—
London Bible Warehouse
PO Box 123
Basingstoke
Hants RG23 7NL

Name: ....
Address: ....
....
....
....

I am especially interested in:—

Music/Theology/"Popular"
Paperbacks
Delete which do not apply